G. Schirmer's Editions
of
Oratorios and Cantatas

THE CREATION

An Oratorio

The Music by

JOSEPH HAYDN

Vocal Score
with a Separate Accompaniment
for the Organ or Piano

Arranged by

VINCENT NOVELLO

Ed. 190

G. SCHIRMER, Inc.

DISTRIBUTED BY

HAL•LEONARD
CORPORATION
7777 W. BLUEMOUND RD. P.O. BOX 13819 MILWAUKEE, WI 53213

THE CREATION

CHARACTERS REPRESENTED

GABRIEL	*Soprano*
URIEL	*Tenor*
RAPHAEL	*Bass*
ADAM	*Bass*
EVE	*Soprano*

PART THE FIRST

No. 1. INTRODUCTION
REPRESENTATION OF CHAOS

No. 2. RECITATIVE. *Raphael*
In the beginning God created the heaven and the earth; and the earth was without form, and void; and darkness was upon the face of the deep.

CHORUS
And the Spirit of God moved upon the face of the waters. And God said, Let there be light: and there was light.

RECITATIVE. *Uriel*
And God saw the light, that it was good: and God divided the light from the darkness.

No. 3. AIR
Now vanish before the holy beams
The gloomy shades of ancient night;
The first of days appears.
Now chaos ends, and order fair prevails.
Affrighted fly hell's spirits black in throngs:
Down they sink in the deep abyss
To endless night.

CHORUS
Despairing, cursing rage attends their rapid fall.
A new-created world springs up at God's command.

No. 4. RECITATIVE. *Raphael*
And God made the firmament, and divided the waters which were under the firmament from the waters which were above the firmament: and it was so.

Now furious storms tempestuous rage,
Like chaff, by the winds impelled are the clouds,
By sudden fire the sky is inflamed,
And awful thunders are rolling on high.
Now from the floods in steam ascend reviving showers of rain,
The dreary, wasteful hail, the light and flaky snow.

No. 5. SOLO. *Gabriel*
The marv'lous work behold amaz'd
The glorious hierarchy of heaven;
And to th' ethereal vaults resound
The praise of God, and of the second day.

CHORUS
And to th' ethereal vaults resound
The praise of God, and of the second day.

No. 6. RECITATIVE. *Raphael*
And God said, Let the waters under the heaven be gathered together to one place, and let the dry land appear: and it was so. And God called the dry land Earth, and the gathering of waters called He Seas: and God saw that it was good.

No. 7. AIR
Rolling in foaming billows,
Uplifted, roars the boisterous sea.
Mountains and rocks now emerge,
Their tops among the clouds ascend.
Through th' open plains, outstretching wide,
In serpent error rivers flow.
Softly purling, glides on
Through silent vales the limpid brook.

No. 8. RECITATIVE. *Gabriel*
And God said, Let the earth bring forth grass, the herb yielding seed, and the fruit-tree yielding fruit after his kind, whose seed is in itself, upon the earth: and it was so.

No. 9. AIR
With verdure clad the fields appear,
Delightful to the ravish'd sense;
By flowers sweet and gay
Enhancèd is the charming sight.
Here fragrant herbs their odours shed;
Here shoots the healing plant.

With copious fruit th' expanded boughs are hung;
In leafy arches twine the shady groves;
O'er lofty hills majestic forests wave.

No. 10. RECITATIVE. *Uriel*
And the heavenly host proclaimed the third day, praising God, and saying:

No. 11. CHORUS
Awake the harp, the lyre awake,
And let your joyful song resound.
Rejoice in the Lord, the mighty God;
For He both heaven and earth
Has clothèd in stately dress.

No. 12. RECITATIVE. *Uriel*
And God said, Let there be lights in the firmament of heaven, to divide the day from the night, and to give light upon the earth; and let them be for signs, and for seasons, and for days, and for years. He made the stars also.

No. 13. RECITATIVE. *Uriel*
In splendour bright is rising now the sun,
And darts his rays; a joyful, happy spouse,
A giant proud and glad

To run his measur'd course.
With softer beams, and milder light,
Steps on the silver moon through silent night;
The space immense of th' azure sky
A countless host of radiant orbs adorns.
And the sons of God announcèd the fourth day
In song divine, proclaiming thus His power:

No. 14. CHORUS
The heavens are telling the glory of God,
The wonder of His work displays the firmament;

TRIO. *Gabriel, Uriel, Raphael*
To day that is coming speaks it the day,
The night that is gone to following night.

CHORUS
The heavens are telling the glory of God,
The wonder of His work displays the firmament.

TRIO
In all the lands resounds the word,
Never unperceivèd, ever understood.

CHORUS
The heavens are telling the glory of God,
The wonder of His work displays the firmament.

PART THE SECOND

No. 15. RECITATIVE. *Gabriel*
And God said, Let the waters bring forth abundantly the moving creature that hath life, and fowl that may fly above the earth in the open firmament of heaven.

No. 16. AIR
On mighty pens uplifted soars
The eagle aloft, and cleaves the air
In swiftest flight, to the blazing sun.
His welcome bids to morn the merry lark,
And cooing calls the tender dove his mate.
From ev'ry bush and grove resound
The nightingale's delightful notes;
No grief affectèd yet her breast,
Nor to a mournful tale were tun'd
Her soft, enchanting lays.

No. 17. RECITATIVE. *Raphael*
And God created great whales, and every living creature that moveth; and God blessèd them, saying,
Be fruitful all, and multiply,
Ye wingèd tribes, be multiplied,
And sing on every tree;
Multiply, ye finny tribes,
And fill each wat'ry deep;
Be fruitful, grow, and multiply,
And in your God and Lord rejoice.

No. 18. RECITATIVE. *Raphael*
And the angels struck their immortal harps, and the wonders of the fifth day sung.

No. 19. TERZETTO
Gabriel
Most beautiful appear, with verdure young adorn'd,
The gently sloping hills; their narrow, sinuous veins
Distil, in crystal drops, the fountain fresh and bright.

Uriel
In lofty circles play, and hover, in the air,
The cheerful host of birds; and as they flying whirl,
Their glitt'ring plumes are dy'd as rainbows by the sun.

Raphael
See flashing through the deep in thronging swarms
The fish a thousand ways around.
Upheavèd from the deep, th' immense Leviathan
Sports on the foaming wave.

Gabriel, Uriel, Raphael
How many are Thy works, O God!
Who may their number tell?

No. 20. TRIO AND CHORUS

The Lord is great, and great His might,
His glory lasts for ever and for evermore.

No. 21. RECITATIVE. *Raphael*

And God said, Let the earth bring forth the
living creature after his kind, cattle, and creep-
ing thing, and beast of the earth, after his kind.

No. 22. RECITATIVE. *Raphael*

Straight opening her fertile womb,
The earth obey'd the word,
And teem'd creatures numberless,
In perfect forms, and fully grown.
Cheerful, roaring, stands the tawny lion. With
sudden leap
The flexible tiger appears. The nimble stag
Bears up his branching head. With flying mane,
And fiery look, impatient neighs the noble steed.
The cattle, in herds, already seek their food
On fields and meadows green.
And o'er the ground, as plants, are spread
The fleecy, meek, and bleating flocks.
Unnumber'd as the sands, in swarms arose
The host of insects. In long dimension
Creeps, with sinuous trace, the worm.

No. 23. AIR

Now heaven in fullest glory shone;
Earth smil'd in all her rich attire;
The room of air with fowl is filled;
The water swell'd by shoals of fish;
By heavy beasts the ground is trod:
But all the work was not complete;
There wanted yet that wondrous being,
That, grateful, should God's power admire,
With heart and voice His goodness praise.

No. 24. RECITATIVE. *Uriel*

And God created Man in His own image, in the
image of God created He him; male and female
created He them.
He breathèd into his nostrils the breath of life,
and Man became a living soul.

No. 25. AIR

In native worth and honour clad,
With beauty, courage, strength, adorn'd,
Erect, with front serene, he stands
A man, the lord and king of nature all.
His large and archèd brow sublime
Of wisdom deep declares the seat;
And in his eyes with brightness shines
The soul, the breath and image of his God.
With fondness leans upon his breast
The partner for him form'd,
A woman, fair and graceful spouse.
Her softly smiling, virgin looks,
Of flow'ry spring the mirror,
Bespeak him love, and joy, and bliss.

No. 26. RECITATIVE. *Raphael*

And God saw every thing that He had made,
and behold, it was very good. And the heavenly
choir, in song divine, thus closèd the sixth day:

No. 27. CHORUS

Achievèd is the glorious work;
The Lord beholds it, and is (well) pleas'd.
In lofty strains let us rejoice,
Our song let be the praise of God.

No. 27 A. TRIO

Gabriel and Uriel
On Thee each living soul awaits;
From Thee, O Lord, all seek their food;
Thou openest Thy hand,
And fillest all with good:

Raphael
But when Thy face, O Lord, is hid,
With sudden terror they are struck;
Thou tak'st their breath away,
They vanish into dust:

Gabriel, Uriel, and Raphael
Thou sendest forth Thy breath again,
And life with vigour fresh returns;
Revivèd earth unfolds new strength
And new delights.

No. 27 B. CHORUS

Achievèd is the glorious work;
Our song let be the praise of God.
Glory to His name for ever.
He sole on high exalted reigns.
Hallelujah.

PART THE THIRD

No. 28. INTRODUCTION. Morning

RECITATIVE. *Uriel*

In rosy mantle appears, by music sweet awak'd,
The morning, young and fair.
From heaven's angelic choir
Pure harmony descends on ravish'd earth.
Behold the blissful pair,
Where hand in hand they go: their glowing looks
Express the thanks that swell their grateful
hearts.
A louder praise of God their lips
Shall utter soon; then let our voices ring,
United with their song.

No. 29. DUET. *Adam and Eve*

By Thee with bliss, O bounteous Lord,
Both heaven and earth are stor'd;

This world so great, so wonderful,
Thy mighty hand has fram'd.

CHORUS

For ever blessèd be His power,
His name be ever magnified.

Adam

Of stars the fairest, pledge of day,
That crown'st the smiling morn;
And thou, bright sun, that cheer'st the world,
Thou eye and soul of all:

CHORUS

Proclaim, in your extended course,
Th' almighty power and praise of God.

Eve

And thou that rul'st the silent night,
And all ye starry hosts,
Spread wide and ev'rywhere His praise
In choral songs about.

Adam

Ye mighty elements, by His power
Your ceaseless changes make;
Ye dusky mists, and dewy steams,
That rise and fall thro' th' air:

CHORUS

Resound the praise of God our Lord.
Great His name, and great His might.

Eve

Ye purling fountains, tune His praise,
And wave your tops, ye pines.
Ye plants, exhale, ye flowers, breathe
To Him your balmy scent.

Adam

Ye that on mountains stately tread,
And ye that lowly creep;
Ye birds that sing at heaven's gate,
And ye that swim the stream:

DUET AND CHORUS

Ye creatures all, extol the Lord!
Him celebrate, Him magnify.

Eve and Adam

Ye valleys, hills, and shady woods,
Made vocal by our song,
From morn till eve you shall repeat
Our grateful hymns of praise.

CHORUS

Hail! bounteous Lord! Almighty, hail!
Thy word call'd forth this wondrous frame,
The heavens and earth Thy power adore;
We praise Thee now and evermore.

No. 30. RECITATIVE. *Adam*
Our duty we have now perform'd,
In offering up to God our thanks.

Now follow me, dear partner of my life!
Thy guide I'll be; and every step
Pours new delights into our breasts,
Shows wonders everywhere.
Then may'st thou feel and know the high degree
Of bliss the Lord allotted us,
And with devoted heart His bounties celebrate.

Eve

O thou for whom I am, my help, my shield,
My all, thy will is law to me:
So God our Lord ordains; and from obedience
Grows my pride and happiness.

No. 31. DUET. *Adam and Eve*
Adam
Graceful consort, at thy side
Softly fly the golden hours;
Ev'ry moment brings new rapture,
Ev'ry care is lull'd to rest.

Eve

Spouse adorèd, at thy side
Purest joys o'erflow the heart;
Life and all I have is thine;
My reward thy love shall be.

Adam

The dew-dropping morn, O, how she quickens
all!

Eve

The coolness of even, O, how she all restores!

Adam

How grateful is of fruits the savour sweet!

Eve

How pleasing is of fragrant bloom the smell!

Both

But, without thee, what is to me
The morning dew, the breath of even,
The sav'ry fruit, the fragrant bloom?
  With thee is every joy enhancèd,
  With thee delight is ever new,
  With thee is life incessant bliss;
  Thine, thine it all shall be.

No. 32. RECITATIVE. *Uriel*
O happy pair! and happy e'er to be,
If not, misled by false conceit,
Ye strive at more than granted is,
And more desire to know, than know ye should.

No. 33. CHORUS WITH QUARTET
Sing the Lord, ye voices all,
    Magnify His name thro' all creation,
    Celebrate His power and glory,
  Let His name resound on high.
  Praise the Lord. Utter thanks.
Jehovah's praise for ever shall endure. **Amen**

INDEX

PART THE FIRST

PART THE THIRD

THE CREATION

№ 1. Representation of Chaos.

     Printed in the U. S. A.

2

Nº 2. "In the beginning."
RECIT.

7317

No 3. "Now vanish before the holy beams."

AIR.

7317

pair-ing rage, Des-pair-ing, at-tends their ra-pid fall.

pair-ing, curs-ing rage, Des-pair-ing, at-tends their ra-pid fall.

Des-pair-ing, curs-ing rage ___ at-tends their ra-pid fall.

Des-pair-ing, curs-ing rage at-tends their ra-pid fall.

A new-cre-a-ted world, A new-cre-a-ted

A new-cre-a-ted world, A new-cre-a-ted

A new-cre-a-ted world. A new-cre-a-ted

A new-cre-a-ted world, A new-cre-a-ted

world springs up, springs up at God's com-mand,

world springs up, springs up at God's com-mand,

world springs up, springs up at God's com-mand,

world springs up, springs up at God's com-mand,

sink in the deep a-byss To end - less night.

Des-pair-ing rage. des-

Des-pair-ing, curs - ing rage at-

CHORUS.

Des-pair-ing, curs - ing

Des-pair-ing, curs - ing rage

mezza voce

pair-ing, at-tends their ra-pid fall. A

tends, at-tends their ra-pid fall. A

rage at-tends their ra-pid fall. A

at-tends their ra - pid fall. A

new-cre-a-ted world, A new-cre-a-ted world springs up, springs

new-cre-a-ted world, A new-cre-a-ted world springs up, springs

new-cre-a-ted world, A new-cre-a-ted world springs up, springs

new-cre-a-ted world, A new-cre-a-ted world springs up, springs

Nº 4. "And God made the firmament."

RECIT.

14

Like chaff, by the winds im-pell'd are the clouds,

By sud-den fire the sky is in-

flam'd,

And aw-ful thun-ders are roll - ing on

Nọ 5. "The marv'lous work."

SOLO and CHORUS

Nº 6. "And God said, Let the waters."
RECIT.

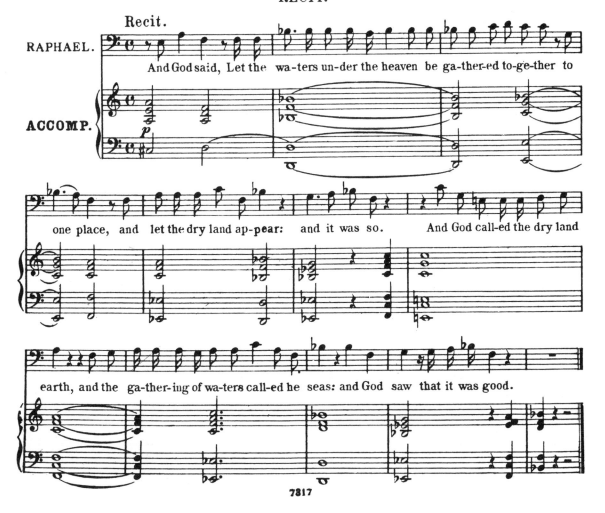

Nº 7. "Rolling in foaming billows."

AIR.

Roll - ing in foam - ing bil - lows, Up - lift - ed, up -

lift - - ed, roars the boist' - rous sea, up - lift - ed

roars the boist' - rous sea. Mountains and rocks now e -

merge, Their tops a - mong the clouds as - cend,

their tops a - mong the clouds as - cend. Mountains and rocks now e -

merge, Their tops a - mong the clouds as - cend, their tops a -

mong the clouds as - cend, a - mong the clouds their tops as -

cend.

Thro' th'o - pen plains out - stretch - - ing wide, In ser - pent

er - ror ri - vers flow. Thro' th'o-pen plains out-

on Thro' si - lent vales the lim - pid

brook, Soft - - ly purl - ing,

glides _____ on Thro' si - - lent vales the

lim - pid brook, Soft - - ly

purl - - ing, glides on Thro' si - lent

Nº 8. "And God said, Let the earth."
RECIT.

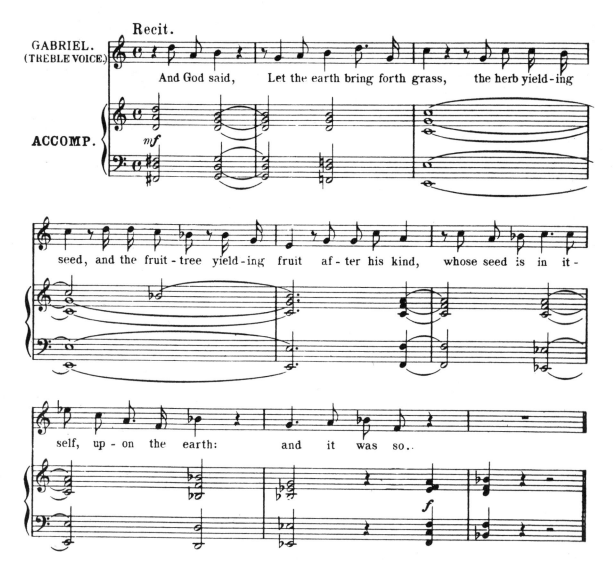

GABRIEL. (TREBLE VOICE.)

And God said, Let the earth bring forth grass, the herb yield-ing

ACCOMP.

mf

seed, and the fruit-tree yield-ing fruit af-ter his kind, whose seed is in it-

self, up-on the earth: and it was so..

f

Nº 9. "With verdure clad."
AIR.

VOICE.

Andante. ♪ = 92.

GABRIEL.

With

ACCOMP.

p *fz* *fz*

ver-dure clad the fields ap-pear, De-light-ful to____ the ra-vish'd sense; By flow-ers

sweet and gay   En-han-ced   is the charm-ing   sight,   En-

han-____-ced   is the charm-ing sight.

Here fra-grant herbs their   o-dours shed; Here shoots the heal-ing

plant, Here shoots____ the heal-ing plant,____

Here shoots the heal-ing plant, ——— the heal-ing plant. ———

Here shoots the heal - -ing plant.

With co - pious fruit th'ex - pand - ed boughs are hung;

In leaf-y arch - es twine the sha - dy groves; O'er

32

7317

Nọ 10. "And the heavenly host."
RECIT.

36

7317

38

7317

- - - - ly dress, in state-ly dress.

state - - - ly dress, in state-ly dress.

- - - - ly dress, in state-ly dress.

- - - - ly dress, in state-ly dress.

Nº 12. "And God said, Let there be lights."

RECIT.

URIEL.

VOICE.

And God said, Let there be lights in the fir-ma-ment of heav'n, to di-

ACCOMP.

vide the day from the night, and to give light upon the earth; And let them be for signs and for

sea-sons, and for days and for years. He made the stars al-so.

Nº 13. "In splendour bright."

RECIT.

Nº14. "The heavens are telling."

CHORUS.

44

7317

word, ne-ver unper-ceiv - ed, e-ver un-der-stood, e-ver, e-ver

ne-ver unper - ceived, e-ver un-der-stood, e-ver, e-ver,

ne-ver unper - ceived, e-ver un-der-stood, e-ver, e-ver,

e - ver un - der - stood.

e - ver un - der - stood.

e - ver un - der - stood.

In all the

In all the lands re - sounds the word. never unper-

lands re - sounds the word, never unper-

In all the lands re - sounds the word, never unper-

7317

50

7317

53

PART THE SECOND.

N⁰ 15. "And God said: Let the waters."

RECIT.

N⁰ 16. "On mighty pens."

AIR.

GABRIEL.

On migh - - ty pens up - lift-ed soars the ea-gle aloft, the ea-gle a-

loft, And cleaves the air in swift - est flight, in swift - est flight to the

blaz - - ing sun, to the blazing sun.

7347

His wel - come bids to morn the merry

lark, His wel - come bids to morn the merry lark;

and coo-ing, and coo-ing

calls the ten - der dove his mate, calls the ten - der dove his mate,

and coo - ing,and coo - ing calls the ten - der

58

dove his mate,   And   cooing, and cooing   calls the tender dove his mate,

calls the ten - - der dove his mate, the ten - - - - -

- - - - der dove his mate,

From ev'_ry   bush ___ and

en - chant - ing,

Her soft, enchanting lays.   No grief af -

fected yet her breast,   Nor to a mournful tale were

tun'd   Her soft, ____   Her soft, ____ enchanting

lays,   Her soft, ____

en - chant - ing lays, Her soft, _____

en - chant - ing lays, Her soft, en - chanting

lays, Her ____ soft, en - chanting lays.

62

№ 17. "And God created great whales."

RECIT.

RAPHAEL.

And God cre - a - ted great whales, and ev'-ry li - ving creature that moveth; and God bless-ed them, say-ing:

Poco adagio. ♩ = 80.

Be fruit-ful all, and mul - ti-ply, Ye wing - ed tribes, be mul - tiplied, and sing on ev'-ry tree;

7317

mul - ti -ply, Ye fin - ny tribes, and fill each wat'-ry deep;

Be fruit-ful, grow, and mul - ti -ply, And

in your God and Lord re - joice, And in your God and Lord re - joice.

Nọ 18. "And the angels."
RECIT.

ad lib.

RAPHAEL.

And the An-gels struck their im-mor-tal harps, and the

ACCOMP.

won-ders, the won -ders of the fifth day sung.

№ 19. "Most beautiful appear."

TERZETTO.

Moderato cantabile. ♪= 84.

GABRIEL. (Treble)

Most beau - ti - ful ap - pear,   With verdure young a -

dorn'd,   The gent - - ly_ slop-ing hills, the gent-ly sloping hills;

Their nar-row, sinuous veins Dis - til, in crystal drops, the

fountain, the foun - tain fresh and bright, Their narrow, sinuous

veins Dis - til, in crys-tal drops, the foun - tain fresh and bright.

URIEL.(Tenor.)

In lof - ty circles play, and ho-ver, in the air. The

cheer - - ful host of birds, the cheerful host of birds; And

68

7317   segue

№ 20. "The Lord is great."

TRIO and CHORUS.

7317

7317

Nᵒ 21. "And God said, let the earth bring forth."

RECIT.

Nᵒ 22. "Straight opening her fertile womb."

RECIT.

stands the tawny li_on.

Presto.

With sudden leap the flexible ti_ger appears.

Presto. ♩.= 112.

The nimble stag bears

up his branching head.

With flying mane, and fiery look, im_patient neighs the noble steed.

№ 23. "Now heav'n in fullest glory shone."

AIR.

The wa - ter swell'd by shoals___ of fish; By hea - vy beasts the ground is trod, By hea - vy beasts the ground is trod: But all the work was not com - plete, But all the

work was not com-plete; There wanted yet that wondrous be - ing,

That grate-ful should God's pow'r ad - mire,

With heart and voice his good - ness praise.

But all the work was not com-plete; There wanted

yet that wond'rous be - ing, That grate - ful should God's pow'r ___ ad -

mire, With heart and voice his good-ness praise,

That grate - ful should God's powr ad -

mire, With heart and voice, With heart,

With heart and voice his good - ness praise,

With heart and voice, With heart and voice his

Nº 24. "And God created man."

RECIT.

URIEL.

And God cre-a-ted Man in his own i-mage, In the i-mage of

ACCOMP.

God cre-a-ted he him; Male and fe-male cre-a-ted he them. He breath-ed

in-to his nostrils the breath of life, and Man be-came a living soul.

№ 25. "In native worth."

AIR.

breath and i - -mage of____ his God.

With fond-ness leans up - on his breast The part-ner for him

form'd, A wo-man, fair and graceful spouse, A woman, fair and grace - ful spouse.

Her soft-ly smiling, vir - gin looks, Of flow'- ry spring the

Nᵒ 26. "And God saw everything that He had made."

RECIT.

92

7817

N.º 27ª "On thee each living soul awaits."
TRIO.

thee each li - ving soul awaits; From thee, O Lord, all seek their food; Thou

thee each li - ving soul awaits; From thee, O Lord, all seek their food; Thou

o - penest thy hand, And fill - est, and fill - est all __ with good:

o - penest thy hand, And fill - est, and fill - est all __ with good:

RAPHAEL.

But when thy face, O Lord! is hid, With sud - den

ter - ror they are struck; Thou

96

7817

98

segue Coro

7317

No 27ᵇ "Achieved is the glorious work."

SECOND CHORUS.

100

102

7317 b

104

7317 b

jah, Hal - le - lu - jah. Glo-ry to his name for e - - ver. He

jah, Hal - le - lu - jah. He sole on high

jah, Hal - le - lu - jah. Glo-ry to his name for e - - ver. He

jah, Hal - le - lu - jah. He sole on high

Org. Ped.

sole on high ex - alt - ed reigns, ex - alt - ed reigns.

ex - alt - ed reigns, ex - alt - ed reigns, ex - alt - ed reigns.

sole on high ex - alt - ed reigns, ex - alt - ed reigns.

ex - alt - ed reigns, ex - alt - ed, reigns, ex - alt - ed reigns.

Hal - le - lu - jah, Hal - le - lu - jah.

Hal - le - lu - jah, Hal - le - lu - jah.

Hal - le - lu - jah, Hal - le - lu - jah.

Hal - le - lu - jah, Hal - le - lu - jah.

End of the second part.

PART THE THIRD.
Nº 28. "In rosy mantle appears."
INTRODUCTION and RECIT.

From heav'n's angel-ic choir Pure har-mo-ny de-scends on ravish'd earth. Behold the blissful pair, where hand in hand they go: their glowing looks ex-press the thanks that swell their grateful hearts. A louder praise of God their lips shall utter soon; Then let our voices ring, u - nited with their song.

№ 29. "By thee with bliss."
DUET and CHORUS.

110

7317

112

7317

Nº 29. (continued) "Of stars the fairest."
DUET and CHORUS.

EVE.
And thou that rul'st the si-lent night, — and all ye star-ry host, —

spread wide, and ev'- ry-where spread

wide his praise in cho - ral songs — a - bout,

spread wide _____ and ev'- ry-where his praise

in cho - ral songs — a - bout.

ADAM.
Ye mighty e - lements,

118

7317

scent.　　　　Ye plants, ex-hale, ye flow - ers, breathe,

breathe to Him_____ your balm - y scent.

ADAM.

Ye　　　　that on

mountains stately tread,　and　ye　　　that low-ly creep;

Ye,　　　ye birds that sing_____ at hea-ven's

gate,　　　And　ye　　　that swim the stream:

brate, him magni - fy, Him, ___ him ce -le - brate, Him, ___ him magni - fy.

brate, him magni - fy, Him, ___ him ce -le - brate, Him, ___ him magni - fy.

brate, him magni - fy, Him, ___ him ce -le - brate, Him, ___ him magni - fy.

brate, him magni - fy, Him, ___ him ce -le - brate, Him, ___ him magni - fy.

brate, him magni - fy, Him, ___ him ce -le - brate, Him, ___ him magni - fy.

brate, him magni - fy, Him, ___ him ce -le - brate, Him, ___ him magni - fy.

EVE.

Ye val - leys,

ADAM.

Ye val - leys,

hills, and sha - dy woods, made vo-cal by our song,

hills, and sha - dy woods, made vo-cal by our song,

124

Nọ 30. "Our duty we have now performed."

RECIT. (ADAM and EVE.)

us, And with de - vo - ted heart His boun-ties ce - le - brate. Come,

come, fol-low me, fol-low me! Thy guide I'll be. O thou for whom I

EVE.

am, my help, my shield, My all, thy will is law to me:

Andante. ♩ =72.

So God our Lord or - dains: and from o - bedience and from o-

be - dience Grows my pride_____ and hap - pi - ness.

№ 31. "Graceful consort."

DUET.   (ADAM and EVE.)

con - sort, Ev'-ry __ moment brings new rap-ture, Ev'-ry care is lull'd to

EVE.

Spouse __ a - do-red, at thy side __ rest.

Pu - rest joys o'er-flow the heart: Life and all I have,

all I __ have is thine; My re - ward, __ My re-

ward thy love __ shall be. __ Spouse a - do - red, Life and

142

7317

№ 32. "O happy pair."
RECIT.

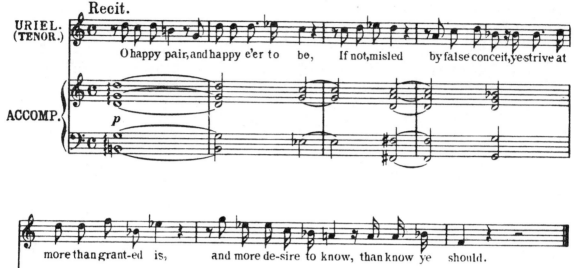

O happy pair, and happy e'er to be, If not, misled by false conceit, ye strive at

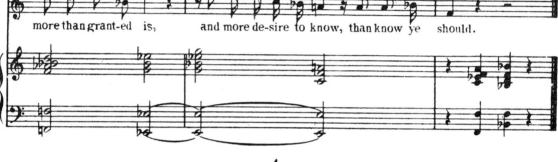

more than grant-ed is, and more de-sire to know, than know ye should.

1

№ 33. "Sing the Lord, ye voices all."
CHORUS with QUARTET.

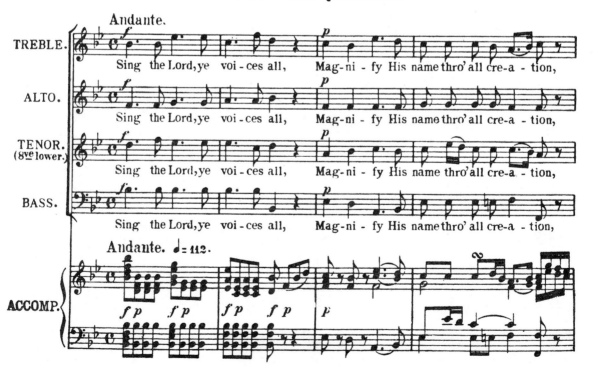

Sing the Lord, ye voi-ces all, Mag-ni-fy His name thro' all cre-a-tion,

152

7317 a

7317 a